W9-ASC-714

BIOGRAPHIES

POCAHONTAS
PEACEMAKER AND FRIEND TO THE COLONISTS

Written by Pamela Hill Nettleton
Illustrated by Jeff Yesh

Special thanks to our advisers for their expertise:

Melodie J. Andrews, Ph.D.
Professor of Early American History
Mankato State University, Mankato, Minnesota

Susan Kesselring, M.A., Literacy Educator
Rosemount–Apple Valley–Eagan (Minnesota) School District

PICTURE WINDOW BOOKS
MINNEAPOLIS, MINNESOTA

Managing Editor: Bob Temple
Creative Director: Terri Foley
Editor: Peggy Henrikson
Editorial Adviser: Andrea Cascardi
Copy Editor: Laurie Kahn
Page production: The Design Lab
The illustrations in this book were rendered digitally.

PICTURE WINDOW BOOKS
5115 Excelsior Boulevard
Suite 232
Minneapolis, MN 55416
1-877-845-8392
www.picturewindowbooks.com

Printed in the United States of America.

Library of Congress Cataloging-in-Publication Data
Nettleton, Pamela Hill.
Pocahontas : peacemaker and friend to the colonists / written by Pamela Hill Nettleton ;
illustrated by Jeff Yesh.
p. cm. — (Biographies)
Summary: A brief biography that highlights some important events in the life of the
woman who helped to bring about peace and friendship between English settlers in
Virginia and the native Powhatan people. Includes bibliographical references and index.
ISBN 1-4048-0187-1
1. Pocahontas, d. 1617–Juvenile literature. 2. Powhatan women–Biography–Juvenile
literature. 3. Smith, John, 1580–1531–Juvenile literature. 4. Jamestown (Va.)–History–
Juvenile literature. 5. Virginia–History–Colonial period, ca. 1600–1775–Juvenile
literature. [1. Pocahontas, d. 1617. 2. Powhatan Indians–Biography. 3. Indians of North
America–Biography. 4. Women–Biography. 5. Jamestown (Va.)–History.] I. Yesh, Jeff,
1971– ill. II. Title.
E99.P85 P5754 2004
975.5′01′092–dc21   2003004116

Pocahontas was the daughter of a Native American chief. She lived about 400 years ago, when the English were first settling America. The English settlers were called colonists. Young Pocahontas was very kind to the colonists of Jamestown, Virginia.

She helped them survive winter in the new land. She was wise and wanted peace between her people and the colonists.

This is the story of Pocahontas.

Pocahontas was born around 1595. She was the daughter of Powhatan, a chief of the Powhatan people. Her mother was one of Powhatan's many wives.

VIRGINIA

Chesapeake Bay

The Powhatans lived in the area around the Chesapeake Bay in what became the colony of Virginia.

Pocahontas's real name was Matoaka. Pocahontas was a nickname that means "spoiled child." Perhaps because she was lively and playful, she got a lot of attention.

Pocahontas may have seen white people for the first time in 1607, when she was about 12 years old. Colonists sailed from England and landed at Jamestown, Virginia.

One of these colonists was Captain John Smith.
Pocahontas and Captain Smith became good friends.

Later Captain Smith wrote that the Powhatans tried to kill him. He said Pocahontas saved his life. He probably made up the story, but it still is being told.

Pocahontas visited the fort at Jamestown often. She came with some of her people and brought the colonists food and furs during the cold winter. In return, the colonists gave the Powhatans things they needed, such as hatchets to chop wood.

Captain Smith said that without Pocahontas the colonists might have starved to death.

In spite of the kindness of Pocahontas, the colonists and the Powhatans soon began to fight with one another. Pocahontas heard that Captain Smith was dead. This news made her very sad.

One of the colonists tricked Pocahontas into getting onto a ship in the harbor. The colonists would not let her leave the ship. They wanted her father to send food.

Pocahontas was not happy about being kidnapped,
but soon she learned to get along with the colonists.
They were kind to her and took her to live
in a new settlement. She married a
successful farmer named John Rolfe.

The marriage helped bring peace between the Powhatans and colonists, but Chief Powhatan never saw his daughter again.

In 1616, Pocahontas sailed to England with some colonists and Powhatans. They wanted to get money for the colonies. Pocahontas's husband and their young son, Thomas, went along.

Pocahontas met the king and the royal family. She even saw her old friend Captain John Smith. He wasn't dead after all! Pocahontas was so shocked she couldn't speak.

The English called
Pocahontas an Indian
princess. Lots of people
talked about her.

Pocahontas helped the English learn about the lives of the colonists in America.

She helped both the English and the colonists learn about her people, the Powhatans. She also taught her people about the white people.

In 1617, John Rolfe decided to return to Virginia with Pocahontas and their son. While getting ready to leave England, Pocahontas became very sick and died. She was only about 22 years old.

Pocahontas was buried in a churchyard in England. Her son, Thomas, later went to school in England. He then moved back to Virginia.

Pocahontas is remembered for being kind and wise. For years, she kept peace between the colonists and her people. She helped Jamestown survive.

THE LIFE OF POCAHONTAS

1595   Born around this year

1607   Saw white men for the first time and met Captain John Smith

1612   Was tricked into boarding an English ship and was held captive. Stayed with the English colonists.

1614   Married colonist John Rolfe

1616   Traveled to England to help raise money for the colonists

1617   Died at about 22 and was buried in England

Did You Know?

- Originally, the name Pocahontas was pronounced POH-kuh-HON-thus.

- Pocahontas's father, Powhatan, lived several miles from Jamestown at a place the Powhatans called Werowocomoco.

- The Jamestown colonists did not know what plants to eat or water to drink in the new land, so they got sick. Pocahontas showed them what to eat and drink to feel better.

- Pocahontas was told that Captain Smith was dead, but he had really only been hurt in a gunpowder explosion. He left America and returned to England. She did not see him until she went to England, eight years later.

- A statue of Pocahontas stands in Virginia where the settlement of Jamestown used to be. The statue shows Pocahontas dressed more like the Native Americans who lived on the plains than those who lived in Virginia.

- There were not many written records when Pocahontas was living. It is hard to know which parts of her story are true and which never happened. The Walt Disney movie about Pocahontas is a fun story, but much of it was made up.

Glossary

colonist (KOL-uh-nist)—someone living in a colony or a land that is newly settled

colony (KOL-uh-nee)—a group of people living in a new land who still are ruled by the country from which they came. Early American colonies were ruled by England.

fort (FORT)—a place built to be strong to keep the people living there safe from attack. A fort had high walls around it.

kidnap (KID-nap)—to capture someone and hold that person until you get what you want. Kidnapping is against the law.

royal (ROI-uhl)—having to do with a king or queen. The royal family is the family of the king and queen.

settlement (SET-uhl-muhnt)—a group of people living in a new village or area. Early settlements in America were often inside forts to protect them.

To Learn More

At the Library

Jenner, Caryn. *The Story of Pocahontas.* New York: Dorling Kindersley Publishing, 2000.

Penner, Lucille Recht. *The True Story of Pocahontas.* New York: Random House, 2003.

Raatma, Lucia. *Pocahontas.* Minneapolis: Compass Point Books, 2002.

Schaefer, Lola M. *Pocahontas.* Mankato, Minn.: Pebble Books, 2002.

On the Web

THE ASSOCIATION FOR THE PRESERVATION OF VIRGINIA ANTIQUITIES

The story of Pocahontas, showing an English painting of her

http://www.apva.org/history/pocahont.html

COLONIAL NATIONAL HISTORICAL PARK

Educational, self-guided activities around "Old Jamestowne," including a link that shows the statue of Pocahontas

http://www.nps.gov/colo/TEACHERS/SG_Act/ SGIndex.htm

FACT HOUND

Fact Hound offers a safe, fun way to find Web sites related to this book. All of the sites on Fact Hound have been researched by our staff.

http://www.facthound.com

1. Visit the Fact Hound home page.
2. Enter a search word related to this book, or type in this special code: 1404801871.
3. Click on the FETCH IT button.

Your trusty Fact Hound will fetch the best sites for you!

On a Trip

HISTORIC "OLD JAMESTOWNE"

Colonial National Historical Park

P.O. Box 210

Yorktown, VA 23690

(757) 898-2411 or (757) 229-1733

http://www.nps.gov/colo/TEACHERS/SG_Act/ SGIndex.htm

Index

birth date of Pocahontas, 4, 22
England, 6, 14, 18–19, 22, 23
English, 3, 15, 16–17, 22
food, 8–9, 11
Jamestown, 3, 6, 8–9, 21, 23

Matoaka, 5
Native American, 3, 23
Powhatan, 4, 11, 13, 23
Powhatan people, 4, 7, 9, 10, 13, 16, 23
Rolfe, John, 12, 14, 18–19, 22

Rolfe, Thomas, 14, 19
Smith, John, 7, 9, 10, 14, 22, 23
statue of Pocahontas, 23
Virginia, 3, 6, 19, 23

4/05